In the In-Between: Teaching in the TCK World

JENI WARD & KATH WILLIAMS

First Edition 2025

© COPYRIGHT INTERWOVEN 2025

All rights reserved. No part of this publication may be reproduced, stored in a retrieval system, or transmitted in any form or by any means (electronic, mechanical, photocopying, recording, or otherwise) without the prior written permission of the publisher.

This book is sold on the condition that it shall not, by way of trade or otherwise, be lent, resold, hired out, or otherwise circulated without the publisher's prior consent, in any form of binding or cover other than that in which it is published, and without a similar condition—including this condition—being imposed on any subsequent purchaser.

ISBN (paperback):

This edition was published in Aberfoyle Park by Mission Interlink in November 2025.

Illustrations:
River by Emma Elliot, page 10

Scripture quoted from the ESV® Bible (The Holy Bible, English Standard Version®), copyright © 2001 by Crossway Bibles, a publishing ministry of Good News Publishers. Used by permission. All rights reserved. Bible passage reference from the NET Bible®, copyright.

Typesetting: Kath Williams

Endorsements

This guide promotes healthy self-awareness, others-awareness, and cultural-awareness in a way that is meaningful, gentle, and manageable for those in transition. It encourages and equips teachers not to require TCKs to check their life stories at the threshold of the classroom but instead to consider their influence holistically—creating depth, healing, and beauty for everyone involved.

At its heart, this purposeful and relevant guide reminds us that as teachers overseas, we can't erase what makes students feel different or disconnected, but we can create community where every child is seen, heard, and valued just as they are. Our classrooms can become places of true belonging—even for those who feel they belong nowhere else.

Lindsay Nimmon TCK Care Coordinator- Teach Beyond

I've just read The In-Between: Teaching in the TCK World and I already want to introduce it to teachers everywhere. Third Culture Kids - those who grow up in contexts away from the home culture of their parents - have particular needs and vulnerabilities which are often unseen and ignored. Teaching in an international setting is both life-enhancing and professionally fulfilling, but it can be fraught with cultural potholes for those unprepared to look out for them.

This easy-to-read interactive workbook encourages its readers to engage reflectively and personally on issues and assumptions around cross-cultural teaching and learning. I believe it could be a valuable professional learning manual for all teachers and trainee teachers, providing wise advice from two who have much experience in, and evidence-based knowledge of, the TCK world.

Sandra Scott Global Connect Ambassdor - Global Connect

I highly recommend this book to anyone who is taking their first steps towards teaching in a cross-cultural setting, as it's designed to open your eyes to the precious gift that awaits you: the gift of working with TCK's.

This book is written as a practical manual; it provides a framework for self-reflection pre-depature and also while in your "new" country.

It also provides many examples of things you can do to build good relationships, trust and stability, in a transient setting. I believe that by working through this book you will be better prepared to go, and be one of the loving, compassionate, and trustworthy teachers that so many TCK's need.

Melanie Martens,
Primary school teacher and private tutor - Australia, Cambodia, Germany

Contents

Table of Contents

About Us 6
Introduction 7
How to Use This Book 8

Part 1: Before You Go 9

Section 1: Know Yourself – Cultural Reflection & Personal Assumptions 10
Section 2: Understanding Third Culture Kids (TCKs) 16
Section 3: Emotional Resilience, Loss, and Grief 23
Section 4: Faith, Identity & Spiritual Formation 31
Section 5: Flexibility and Contextual Norms 38
Section 6: Your Influence as a Teacher 45

Part 2: While You Are Overseas 51

Section 7: Building Meaningful and Safe Connections 53
Section 8: Creating Space for Belonging 59
Section 9: Navigating Transitions & Goodbyes 65
Section 10: Caring for Yourself 72

Conclusion: Teaching Beyond Borders 79

Resources and Recommended Reading 83

About us

INTERWOVEN

Interwoven is a Missions Interlink Ministry, created through a partnership of dedicated workers with a passion for nurturing Third Culture Kids, ensuring their physical, spiritual, and mental well-being on the field. Our primary mission is to develop resources that directly engage Third Culture Kids. Additionally, we aim to support and provide valuable resources to those who work with and care for them.

KATH WILLIAMS

Kath is a dedicated social worker passionate about supporting Third Culture Kids (TCKs) in their growth and development. She currently works with TCKs through two mission organizations in Australia and co-authored Navigating a Global Transition Again: A Journey of Faith and Thongs or Flip Flops: A Book for Aussie TCKs.

With over 20 years of experience with children and teens, Kath has worked with Indigenous communities, foster children, and community camps, and spent two years in Cambodia supporting students at Hope International School and mentoring youth at a local international church.

Beyond her work, Kath enjoys coffee with friends, photography, visiting zoos, reading, music, and traveling whenever she can.

JENI WARD

Jeni Ward is a Third Culture Kid (TCK) whose journey has taken her across Ethiopia, South Sudan, Canada, and Australia. With over 13 years of experience in cross-cultural ministry, she is dedicated to understanding and bridging cultural gaps while walking alongside other TCKs to offer guidance, support, and community.

A founding member of Interwoven, Jeni has been instrumental in developing materials and resources for TCKs, including God in the Mess, God in the Cracks, and Navigating a Global Transition Again: A Journey of Faith (co-authored with Kath Williams). Through her work with Interwoven and in her everyday life, Jeni's passion for connecting, inspiring, and empowering others shines through her coaching and debriefing work.

Introduction

Teaching in a New Culture Begins with Who You Are

You've been called, appointed, or perhaps simply curious, stepping into a classroom far from home, ready to teach students whose stories may stretch across continents. Whether you're serving in a mission-based school, an international institution, or a multicultural learning environment, one thing is sure:
- You are not just bringing knowledge—you're bringing yourself.
- Your accent, your values, your assumptions about how learning should happen and how faith should be shared.
- Your idea of what children should be like.
- Your hidden expectations of what life overseas will feel like.
- Your faith.
- Your fears.
- Your hopes.

This guide was written to help you slow down, reflect, and prepare well, not just for the logistics of moving abroad, but for the transformation that happens when we truly engage across cultures.

What This Book Is (and Isn't)
This is not a how-to manual or a doctrinal checklist.

It's a reflective, practical, and profoundly human resource created to help you:
- Understand the complex lives of Third Culture Kids (TCKs)
- Examine your cultural and spiritual expectations.
- Explore the significance of faith, resilience, and connection in a global classroom.
- Learn to teach with humility, flexibility, and integrity.
- Take care of your students and yourself.

You won't find all the answers in these pages. But you will find questions worth asking before you go, and while you are there.

How to Use This Book

The content is structured in two parts:

Part 1: Before You Go

Foundational insights, reflection activities, and cultural orientation tools to help you prepare with eyes wide open.

Part 2: While You Are Overseas

On-the-ground support for relational care, emotional awareness, faith integration, and sustainable teaching practice.

You can work through this book alone, with a team, or in a mentoring context. It's designed to be interactive—write in the margins, answer the prompts, and return to it again when culture shock hits or the connections feel hard to build.

> 🌍 **Why This Matters**
>
> As you enter this space, you're among students who are navigating change, discovering their identities, or coping with quiet struggles. You don't need to be flawless to make a difference. What's more important is being aware, present, and genuine.
>
> "You won't just be remembered for what you taught. You'll be remembered for how you made them feel seen, known, and safe."
>
> Welcome to the journey.

Part 1: Before You Go

Section 1: Know Yourself – Cultural Reflection & Personal Assumptions

Know Yourself – Cultural Reflection & Personal Assumptions

"You don't arrive empty-handed. But you don't arrive finished, either."

Before diving into a new culture, take a moment to reflect on the culture you're bringing with you. Your background, values, routines, and preconceptions will influence how you make sense of your new surroundings, both in everyday life and in the classroom.

This section is meant to help you examine your worldview before you're swept up in someone else's. The more aware you are of your own biases, the better you'll be at responding with empathy and humility.

Why Self-Awareness Matters
It's not just about crossing borders – you're navigating different worldviews.

TCKs and local students are constantly adapting to new systems, expectations, and relationships.

The more aware you are of your own biases, the better you'll be at responding with empathy and humility.

Reflection: Your Cultural Framework

✍Your Turn: Reflect & Respond

"If you want to teach cross-culturally, begin by learning your own culture deeply."

Ask yourself:
- What did your culture teach you about authority, success, and independence?

- How do you define "respect"? What do you assume it looks like?

- How do you naturally handle conflict, grief, and silence?

- What's your internal reaction to religious or political views that differ from yours?

Practical Orientation: Everyday Expectations
"What assumptions do you have about daily life? Be honest.

What assumptions do you have about daily life? Be honest.
What do you expect your first home to be like?
Do you assume you'll have air-conditioning, quiet neighbours, or privacy?
How do you expect to shop, cook, or travel?
What do you imagine local kids will be like?
What's your image of a "normal" school day?

These assumptions aren't inherently right or wrong, but unexamined expectations can lead to frustration, culture shock, and missed opportunities for connection.

🌎 Why This Matters

When you know what you expect, you can notice when those expectations clash with reality.

This awareness helps you respond with curiosity instead of criticism — and humility instead of disappointment.

✍️ Cultural & Lifestyle Audit Worksheet

Now that you've identified your assumptions, take a moment to explore how they show up in daily life. The following worksheet helps you recognize where your cultural defaults might meet a new reality and how to stay open when they do.

Area	My Expectation/Belief	Where It Comes From	How I'll Stay Flexible
Student Behaviour	"Kids should sit still and listen."	My schooling	Explore norms for discipline locally
Grocery Shopping	"A good store has everything in one place."	Convenience culture	Ask locals where they shop and why
Faith Conversations	"Sharing faith should be open and direct."	Church community	Observe local norms first
Free Time	"Weekends are for rest and personal space."	Personal preference	Expect relational culture to differ
Discipline/Respect	"Kids should respond to authority immediately"	Teaching background	Learn how respect is expressed here

✍️ Your Turn: Reflect & Respond

These prompts are meant to be journaled slowly perhaps one per day, or discussed with your mentor or team.

- What do I assume about the "right" way to teach?

- How might my view of respect, discipline, or communication be misunderstood?

- When do I feel most out of control, and how do I react?

- What's something I hope will be the same—and how will I handle it if it's not?

> 🌱 **Final Thought**
>
> Start by becoming a student of yourself. The more clarity you have about your beliefs and habits, the more capacity you'll have to honour someone else's.
>
> *"If you want to teach cross-culturally, begin by learning your own culture deeply."*
>
> Return to this page after your first month abroad.
> - What assumptions proved true?
> - Which ones surprised you?

Section 2: Understanding Third Culture Kids (TCKs)

Understanding Third Culture Kids (TCKs)
Before You Teach Globally, Understand Who's in the Room.

"Belonging everywhere—and nowhere—all at once."
— Common experience of TCKs

Don't expect to find "TCK" in a student's file. But you'll likely meet students who've lived in three or more countries before turning ten… who switch languages mid-conversation… who carry their grief in silence… or who are much more mature than they seem.

These are Third Culture Kids (TCKs) — students who live in between worlds, often without a clear sense of home to call their own. Understanding their identity and experiences is crucial for anyone preparing to teach in international or globally mobile contexts.

🌍 Why This Matters

TCKs often embody both privilege and loss. Their lives can look worldly and confident, yet carry deep experiences of transition and hidden grief.

To teach them well, you must understand what shapes them — the movements, the goodbyes, the richness, and the ache of belonging everywhere and nowhere.

You are not just teaching across cultures; you are teaching in between them.

What Is a TCK?

Third Culture Kids are children who have spent a significant part of their early years living outside their parents' country of origin.

The term Third Culture Kid was first coined by sociologists Dr. Ruth Van Reken and Dr. David Pollock, who observed children growing up in cultures different from their parents'. Over time, it's come to describe globally mobile children who form a "third culture" that blends elements of all the places they've lived.

The "third culture" isn't the passport culture or the host culture, but rather the shared, in-between experience of people who have lived internationally and carried multiple cultural influences at once.

Examples include:
- Children of missionaries, military personnel, diplomats, or NGO staff
- Mixed-heritage or bi-national students
- Children who've moved across countries multiple times during childhood

Though TCKs are found through all the world's cultures they have a shared global identity that goes beyond just a blend of the cultures they have been influenced by. In the above image this is represented by the cloud that is the Third culture being the same even when the TCKs are found in the context different world cultures.

✺ Core Characteristics of TCKs

Strengths	Challenges
Adaptable, flexible in new environments	Lack of rootedness or a lasting sense of home
Mature and insightful	Feel pressure always to be "okay"
Relationally deep and intuitive	Struggle with constant goodbyes
Multilingual or culturally fluent	Feel misunderstood by mono-cultural peers
Globally minded	Can become disconnected from a specific identity
Quick learners and keen observers	May over-adapt or mirror others to fit in
Comfortable in diverse groups	Uncertain how to answer "Where are you from?"
Empathetic and emotionally intelligent	Tend to internalise grief or minimise emotions
Independent, self-reliant problem solvers	Difficulty asking for help or showing vulnerability
Able to build bridges across cultures	Can experience loyalty conflicts between cultures or beliefs
Creative and open-minded thinkers	Can feel like "outsiders" everywhere — even at home
Resilient and resourceful	Resilience sometimes mistaken for emotional health

💬 Teacher Insight

TCKs often carry the same tension that makes cross-cultural life so beautiful — the capacity to connect widely, and the ache of belonging nowhere fully.

In your classroom, you may see this as both confidence and withdrawal, enthusiasm and fatigue, maturity and quiet sadness sometimes in the same day.

TCK Identity & Belonging

TCKs often wrestle with questions like:

> "Where am I from?"
> "Who understands me?"
> "Why do I feel so out of place — everywhere?"

They can feel like outsiders everywhere — even in places built for people like them. Their sense of belonging is relational, not geographical.

They feel like they belong when they are understood.

📖 How to Prepare as a Teacher

As a teacher, you are entering the world of children who have had to start over — again and again.

Your posture matters as much as your pedagogy. The best preparation is not about strategy, but about cultivating humility, consistency, and listening hearts.

Learn the Basics
- TCKs aren't defined by where they're from, but by how they've lived.
- Don't assume familiarity with local pop culture or traditions.
- Be cautious with labels — TCKs are individuals, not stereotypes.

Build a Trust Bridge
- Trust takes time. Many TCKs have learned to keep their guard up.
- Start by listening. Be curious, not intrusive.
- Don't expect their vulnerability before you've earned it.

Make Space for Identity Exploration
- Use world maps, timelines, or cultural collages.
- Allow multiple answers to "Where are you from?"
- Be comfortable with ambiguity — it's their norm.

Pre-Departure Reflection for Teachers

Take time to journal through these prompts — or discuss them with a mentor or team. Don't rush your answers; they may reveal assumptions that shape your teaching more than you realize.

Ask yourself:

In what ways am I prepared — or unprepared — to support students who don't fit into neat cultural categories?

How might I respond when a student shows grief, distance, or guardedness, and what could that reveal about their experiences?

How willing am I to learn from students who may bring broader cultural awareness or international experience than I do?

What assumptions might I need to let go of in order to see each student as a unique individual?

🌱 Final Thought:

See the Story, Not Just the Student

Every TCK walks into your classroom with a layered story — full of beauty, ache, insight, and adaptation.
Your job isn't to define them. It's to see them.

"They don't need you to fix their story. They need you to understand that they have one."

Reflection: Before you teach, pause and ask yourself: Am I ready to listen before I lead?

Section 3: Emotional Resilience, Loss and Grief

Emotional Resilience, Loss & Grief
Understanding the Inner World of Students Who Are Globally Mobile

> "They might not say it, but they feel it."
> — TCK Mentor

Third Culture Kids are often praised for their ability to adapt. They're masters at fitting in, making new friends, and thriving in unfamiliar situations.
But adaptability is not the same as resilience.

Resilience isn't just coping with change it's learning how to grow through it. It's about having space, language, and support to process what's been lost, not just push forward.

In this section, you'll learn to recognize the invisible weight many globally mobile students carry — and how to help them develop the emotional grounding they need to thrive, not just survive.

🌍 Why This Matters

Frequent transitions can make TCKs look resilient on the outside, but inwardly they may feel fragmented, lonely, or numb.
As a teacher, your calm presence and consistent care can become an anchor point helping them learn that belonging isn't tied to a place, but to people who stay when everything else changes.

You can't prevent their goodbyes, but you can help them say them well.

What Is Emotional Resilience?

Resilience is the capacity to bounce back from challenges not by pretending everything is fine, but by working through pain in a safe and supported environment.

For TCKs, emotional resilience involves navigating:
- Constant transitions and goodbyes
- Repeated identity shifts
- Feelings of loneliness, disconnection, or rootlessness
- Culture shock and reverse culture shock
- Academic pressure in new systems

Many TCKs appear "fine" high-achieving, polite, well-behaved. Yet this surface calm often masks exhaustion, confusion, or quiet grief. What looks like strength can sometimes be survival.

The Goodbye Culture

"TCKs say more goodbyes by age 18 than many monocultural adults say in a lifetime."

Goodbye is woven into the rhythm of a TCK's life. Each move can mean saying farewell to:
- Best friends
- Homes, pets, and favorite places
- Languages and routines
- Spiritual communities or church families
- Entire seasons of identity

These goodbyes are often:
- Unexpected – with little time to prepare
- Downplayed – "You'll make new friends!"
- Unseen – no clear rituals or closure
- Stacked – with little time to grieve before the next move

Without space to process, grief can build up quietly — showing up later as detachment, perfectionism, over-achievement, or emotional withdrawal.

Familiar Sources of Grief in TCKs

Loss of place and possessions
Homes, pets, favorite toys, familiar streets — even the smell of local food or the sound of neighborhood life can carry deep meaning.

"Every move means leaving behind a world they had just started to belong to."

Loss of relationships
Friends, mentors, and extended family members are left behind with each move. Online connections help, but time zones and new routines often make them fade.

"Every goodbye is another small grief they learn to silence."

Loss of stability and predictability
Schedules, traditions, and routines constantly change. A new school means new systems, new rules, new expectations — sometimes every few years.

This can lead to hyper-vigilance, over-control, or burnout from constant adjustment.

Loss of language or cultural fluency

A child fluent in one language or accent may lose it after moving. Humor, idioms, or unspoken rules of behavior may no longer "fit."

Language loss often feels like losing part of oneself.

Missing life events back "home"

Birthdays, holidays, funerals, weddings, family milestones — they happen without them.

> Watching these moments through photos or screens deepens the sense of distance.

Burnout from always being "the one who adjusts"

TCKs learn early to adapt and perform — to blend in, to be fine. Over time, that can lead to emotional fatigue, suppressed grief, and an identity built around strength instead of honesty.
> "Adaptability becomes armor."

Loss of belonging or identity anchor

Each new environment requires redefinition: Who am I here? What rules apply? Where do I fit?
> Without deep roots, belonging becomes relational — and fragile.

💬 Teacher Insight

When students seem unusually composed or "mature beyond their years," remember what they may have learned: that showing sadness only makes goodbyes harder.

Create a classroom where laughter, silence, and tears all have a place. This doesn't weaken learning — it deepens it.

Many TCKs can't yet name what they've lost; they've never been given permission to grieve. Your empathy becomes the language they didn't know they could speak.

📖 How Teachers Can Support Resilience

As a teacher, you are entering the world of students who have had to start over again and again.

Your posture matters as much as your pedagogy. Support isn't about fixing feelings; it's about making space for them.

Acknowledge Transitions
- Honour moments of arrival and departure.
- Use rituals like memory circles, farewell notes, or "transition walls."
- Celebrate the stories that each student carries.

Make Space for Emotion

- Normalise emotional check-ins.
- Let students feel multiple emotions at once — joy, sadness, relief, anger — without judgment.

Teach Emotional Language

- Help students name what they're feeling ("sad but thankful," "excited yet scared").
- Use books, art, metaphors, or physical movement to express complex emotions.

Be a Stable Adult

- Offer predictability and reliability.
- Communicate clearly about your plans and presence — your stability helps theirs.

Toolbox: Classroom Resources

Activities
- Loss Map: Students draw or journal about people, places, and moments they've said goodbye to.
- "I Carry With Me…": A writing prompt about what they keep from each place they've lived.
- Emotion Check-Ins: Use colours, emojis, or phrases to help students identify how they feel.
- Gratitude + Grief Journals: "One thing I miss, one thing I'm thankful for."
- Memory Boxes: Invite students to create a small keepsake box for items or symbols from their past homes.
- Use Moody Monsters or Emotional Cards to check in how they are feeling.

Pre-Departure Reflection for Teachers

Take time to explore your own relationship with loss — it will shape how you respond to students who are grieving quietly.

- What was my experience of grief growing up? Was it welcomed or avoided?

- How do I respond to emotional expression — especially tears or silence?

- Am I more comfortable with compliance than authenticity?

- How can I prepare to support students who may not verbalize their pain?

- What's one way I could acknowledge goodbyes better in my classroom?

> 🌱 **Final Thought:**
>
> Presence Is the Best Curriculum
>
> Third Culture Kids don't need to be rescued from sadness.
> They need you to recognize it — and stay with them in it.
>
> Your presence, consistency, and care especially in the in-between moments can help them build the resilience they'll carry for life.
>
> *"In a world where everything shifts, be the one who stays."*

Section 4: Faith, Identity & Spiritual Formation

Faith, Identity & Spiritual Formation
Navigating the Sacred Tensions of the Global Classroom

"When God is your parents' job, it's easy to feel like you're just part of the brand."
— Adult TCK

In many international and mission-based schools, faith is both central and complicated. Students come with a wide range of spiritual backgrounds, questions, and emotions. Some are curious and open; others are skeptical, weary, or quietly angry.

For teachers, faith is not only a subject it's a presence in the classroom. You bring your own convictions, habits, and assumptions, often shaped by your culture and experience.

This section invites you to examine how you live your faith across cultures and how to engage your students' spiritual journeys with honesty, empathy, and grace.

🌍 Why This Matters

For many Third Culture Kids, faith has been both a foundation and a fracture point. They've seen religion lived in public but questioned in private, preached with passion but practiced inconsistently.

As an educator, you have the sacred opportunity to make faith feel safe again not by having all the answers, but by modeling authenticity, humility, and love that doesn't depend on performance.

Faith for TCKs: Shared, Inherited, or Personal?

Many TCKs grow up surrounded by faith — mission trips, chapel services, Bible lessons but struggle to distinguish between inherited belief and personal conviction.

Their journey might include:
- Faith that is performed publicly, but rarely processed privately
- Ministry life that is interwoven with family life
- Mixed messages about doubt, anger, or spiritual struggle
- Religious language used in place of genuine emotional expression
- Pressure to appear spiritual, especially as "missionary kids"

"Faith should be an invitation — but for many TCKs, it has felt like an obligation."

Tensions You May Encounter

Theme	What It Might Look Like	What's Beneath the Surface
Performance-based faith	Students give correct answers but don't engage deeply	Fear of disappointing adults; shallow or borrowed faith
Spiritual fatigue	Detachment or apathy in chapels or devotions	Overexposure without space to personalize belief
Faith as identity conflict	Students appear resistant or disengaged	Confusion about where family loyalty ends and personal conviction begins
Lack of spiritual safety	Silence in discussions about doubt or sin	Past experiences of judgment, shame, or exclusion
Intellectual disillusionment	"If God is good, why was life so hard?"	Grief, trauma, or perceived hypocrisy in faith communities
Cultural faith clash	Students question mission practices or Western theology	Wrestling with ethnocentrism or cultural imposition in "God language"

> **💬 Teacher Insight**
>
> Faith conversations in global classrooms aren't about controlling outcomes they're about creating safety for wonder and honesty.
>
> When students realize you can handle their doubts without shock or shame, they begin to believe God might be able to handle them too.

📖 How to Prepare Spiritually as a Teacher

As a teacher, your spiritual presence may be the clearest message your students receive about God.

Before you teach theology, live grace.

Reflect on Your Journey

- Where has your culture shaped your beliefs more than Scripture?
- What doubts have you wrestled with — and how do you handle uncertainty?
- How do you engage students who disagree or question your faith perspective?

Model Faith as Relationship, Not Behaviour

- Let students see honesty, struggle, and joy — not perfection.
- Speak of your faith with warmth and humility, not as a performance.
- Avoid rigid formulas or moralising statements that simplify complex realities.

Create Space, Not Pressure

- Never assume all your students are Christians, even in mission schools.
- Invite questions, and allow silence to sit without rushing to fix it.
- Offer spiritual rhythms — prayer, reflection, gratitude as invitations, not expectations.
- Encourage students to explore what faith means for them, not what it must look like for you.

Key Insight: Students May Feel Like the Exception to the Gospel

Some TCKs carry deep, unspoken questions:
- "If God loves me, why did my family's calling make me feel invisible?"
- "If faith is real, why does no one talk about burnout, doubt, or mental health?"
- "Does God see me — or just what I represent to others?"

Your willingness to sit with these questions — without rushing to fix or defend — may reshape how a student understands God's patience and tenderness.

How you listen may reveal more about the heart of God than any lesson you teach.

✍️ Pre-Departure Reflection Prompts

Take time to explore your own relationship with faith before you step into a cross-cultural classroom.

Write, pray, or discuss your responses with a mentor.

- When I was a student, how was faith taught or modeled to me?

- Am I comfortable allowing space for doubt or silence?

- Do I equate spiritual interest with good behaviour or outward enthusiasm?

- How might I unintentionally reinforce performance-based faith?

- What does it look like to be a safe adult who listens without needing to fix?

- When students lose faith, do I respond with fear — or compassion?

> 🌱 **Final Thought:**
>
> Be Someone Who Makes Faith Feel Safe Again
>
> Your role isn't to convince every student to believe as you do it's to model what faith with integrity and gentleness looks like.
>
> For many globally mobile kids, faith has been taught in systems but rarely experienced in safety.
>
> Let your presence remind them that God is patient, personal, and kind.
>
> *"Some students won't remember your devotions but they'll remember how you responded when they whispered, 'I don't know what I believe anymore.'"*

Section 5: Flexibility and Contextual Norms

Flexibility & Contextual Norms
Letting Go of "The Right Way" to Make Room for Many Ways

"Culture is not right or wrong — it's just different. But if you're unaware of your own, you'll assume everyone else is doing it wrong."

For many new international teachers, the biggest challenge isn't lesson planning or packing it's adjusting to the unspoken expectations that shape daily life, relationships, and classroom dynamics.

This section helps you prepare for the reality that what you consider "normal," "respectful," or even "Christian" may look different in your host culture. That's not a threat it's an invitation to grow.

Teaching cross-culturally means learning to see difference not as disobedience, but as diversity.

🌍 Why This Matters

The way people relate, worship, and learn is shaped by culture including yours.
Flexibility in a new context isn't compromise; it's wisdom.
When you adapt your style to local norms, you show humility, build trust, and make space for genuine understanding.

What Are Contextual Norms?

Contextual norms are the shared expectations and unwritten rules that guide:
- How people relate to authority
- What counts as respectful or rude
- How conflict is handled (or avoided)
- Which emotions are acceptable in public
- What defines a "good student" or a "good teacher"
- How faith is practiced and expressed

When your norms clash with someone else's, it doesn't mean they're wrong it means you've entered a different context.

And that means it's your turn to learn the rules.

The Three Cultural Layers Every TCK Navigates

Passport Culture	Host Culture	School Culture
Home or passport country norms (e.g. Korean, Australia)	Local beliefs, traditions, and social expectations	Curriculum, policies, and institutional values
Family values, communication style, and faith traditions	Local gender roles, time orientation, and social cues	Often a blend of international, Western, and mission influences
"We say what we think."	"We avoid confrontation."	"We expect initiative and participation."

TCKs move between these three layers daily.
They may act one way at home, another at school, and another in the local community not because they're inconsistent, but because they're adapting

Teacher Insight

The more you understand these cultural layers, the better you'll interpret student behaviour.

- What looks like disinterest might be respect.
- What feels like confrontation might be honesty.
- What seems like silence might be deep thought.

What This Means for You as a Teacher

When you enter a new culture, you also enter a new system of meaning. Without awareness, your teaching style can be misread as rude, distant, or controlling even when your intentions are good.

Cultural intelligence means learning to see through their lens before judging through your own.

Common Cultural Assumptions to Check

Topic	Western / Individualistic View	Possible Alternate Norm
Respect	Making eye contact, speaking up	Averting eyes, waiting to be invited to speak
Discipline	Independent reflection, explaining why	Obedience is expected without question
Time	Punctuality shows respect	Relationships come before time
Faith	Openly discussing beliefs	Faith is private or expressed through action
Gender Roles	Equal participation expected	Distinct gender expectations shape interactions
Conflict	Address issues directly	Avoid confrontation to maintain harmony
Feedback	Honest and immediate	Indirect, softened to preserve face

Cultural Posture: Flexible, Not Fragile

Flexibility doesn't mean abandoning your values —it means adapting your behaviour so your values can be heard clearly.
You can hold firm convictions and still show cultural humility.
The more flexible you are, the more accessible your message becomes.

📖 Practical Ways to Build Cultural Flexibility

Observe Before Acting
- Spend time watching how local teachers lead, speak, and relate.
- Ask, "What's being communicated here that words don't show?"

Ask Curious Questions
- When something feels uncomfortable or confusing, ask with humility, not frustration.
- "Can you help me understand how this is usually done here?"

Find a Cultural Mentor
- Identify a trusted local colleague who can explain customs or help you interpret misunderstandings.

Pause Before Correcting
- When a student or peer reacts unexpectedly, ask yourself: "Is this about behaviour — or about culture?"

Reframe Success
In cross-cultural teaching, success isn't uniformity — it's mutual understanding.

✍ Pre-Departure Reflection Prompts

Take time to think through your cultural expectations before you go. These reflections will prepare you to listen and adapt with grace.

- How do I define respect, and how might that differ elsewhere?

- What do I assume "good students" do?

- How do I usually handle conflict, and how might that be perceived differently?

- What will I do when a student doesn't respond as I expect?

- Am I willing to adapt how I teach, pray, or lead without compromising my integrity?

- Who could help me understand the local context more deeply?

> 🌱 **Final Thought:**
> You're Not Just a Teacher — You're a Learner Too
>
> Teaching across cultures begins with curiosity.
> You may have come to teach, but you'll find yourself learning daily about people, patience, and perspective.
>
> What works in one classroom may not work in another, not because your method is flawed, but because culture is real.
>
> *"Let your curiosity lead before your judgment speaks."*

Section 6: Your Influence as a Teacher

Your Influence as a Teacher
Living Seen, Leading with Integrity

"You may be one of a hundred adults in a child's life, but they will remember how it felt to be around you."

Teaching overseas especially within mission-based or tight-knit international communities means your life is often more visible than you expect.

Your students see you not only in the classroom, but in the grocery store, at church, online, and in the way you greet your neighbours.

In these settings, how you live often speaks louder than what you teach.
Your presence becomes part of their formation — shaping how they understand trust, leadership, and faith.

You are always communicating something — even in silence, frustration, or rest.

🌍 Why This Matters

In cross-cultural spaces, students and families don't just watch your teaching they watch your life.
They notice how you handle pressure, conflict, or fatigue.
They learn what grace looks like when you make mistakes.

You don't have to be flawless to be influential — you have to be faithful.

You Are Always Teaching — Even When You're Not

In small, globally mobile communities, visibility is constant.
You are seen:
- At church or community gatherings
- At the supermarket or market stalls
- On social media posts and photos
- In how you speak to locals or support staff
- In how you react to delays, exhaustion, or discomfort

Students and parents are not just watching your lessons — they're watching your life.
Your daily example can become the most lasting curriculum they ever experience.

The Hidden Curriculum of Your Presence

What You Do	What They Learn
Admit when you're wrong	Humility is stronger than perfection
Treat others with kindness	Faith is lived, not just spoken
Stay calm in confusion	The unfamiliar can be safe
Ask for help	Adults can be learners too
Honour student privacy	Trust is possible, even across cultures
Apologise sincerely	Grace is not weakness — it's strength

The tone of your life becomes the lesson plan they'll never forget.

> **Teacher Insight**
>
> You teach twice — once with your words, and once with your witness.
> Students will remember your calm more than your curriculum, and your kindness long after your lessons fade.

Leading With Authenticity, Not Image

In cross-cultural work, it's easy to slip into performance mode — to prove your worth through polished faith or perfect professionalism.

But TCKs, more than most, have finely tuned radar for inauthenticity. They've met many adults who said one thing and lived another.

Authenticity builds safety. Consistency builds trust.

You don't have to be impressive — you need to be real.

> *"The faith you live will speak louder than the words you teach."*

Things Students Notice (Even If They Never Say So)

- Whether you're kind to "unimportant" people
- How you speak about the local culture or government
- If you keep your word, even in small things
- Whether you make space for people who are different
- How you talk about other teachers or staff
- If you treat them the same when no one is watching

These moments are the unseen soil of spiritual formation.

📔 Preparing to Live Seen

Know Your Non-Negotiables

- What values and rhythms will anchor you when life feels public?
- Your boundaries and habits protect your integrity.

Set Gentle Boundaries

- Your life is visible, but it doesn't have to be available 24/7.
- Model rest, privacy, and self-care — they teach balance.

Expect Misunderstanding

- Even good intentions can be misread. Choose grace over defensiveness.

Stay Rooted in Accountability

- Find safe mentors or teammates who let you process without judgment.
- Honesty with others will keep you grounded in truth and humility.

✏️ Pre-Departure Reflection Prompts

As you prepare to teach, remember: you're not just entering a school you're stepping into people's stories.

Your influence will come less from your title and more from your tenderness.

- Where in my life am I most tempted to perform instead of be authentic?

- What parts of my personality or routine will feel most exposed in a new context?

- How will I respond when my intentions are misunderstood?

- What habits will keep me emotionally grounded and spiritually honest?

- Am I willing to be visible, humble, and consistent — even when it's uncomfortable?

- Who will I invite into my circle for accountability and prayer?

> 🌱 **Final Thought:**
> Who You Are Is Part of What You Teach
>
> In cross-cultural classrooms, your presence becomes a living curriculum. Students will learn as much from your patience, tone, and truthfulness as from your lessons.
>
> You don't need to be the loudest voice in their lives — just a steady one.
>
> *"In a world of shifting stories and short goodbyes, be the kind of teacher whose faithfulness is remembered long after your title is forgotten."*

Part 2: While You Are Overseas

Teaching With Presence, Wisdom, and Care in a Cross-Cultural World

"Now that you're here, the real learning begins."

Whether you're well-prepared or not, being in-country will still surprise, challenge, and shape you in new ways. You've crossed borders but now you're navigating hallways, relationships, supermarket queues, and the emotional ups and downs. You're meeting students with complex stories, families with unspoken hopes, and cultural rhythms that don't always align with your own.

Here, you'll find advice on tackling the daily challenges of teaching across cultures how to build trust, deal with loss, look after your well-being, and keep growing as an educator and a person.

What This Section Covers:

- **Building Meaningful and Safe Connections**

  (How to build trust with students who may be guarded, grieving, or unsure you'll stay)

- **Creating Space for Belonging**

  (Practical ways to honour culture, identity, and story in your classroom)

- **Navigating Transitions & Goodbyes**

  (How to support students—and yourself—through arrivals, departures, and changes)

- **Caring for Yourself**

  (Sustainable rhythms, healthy boundaries, and self-awareness in emotionally demanding work)

Section 7: Building Meaningful and Safe Connections

Building Meaningful and Safe Connections
Becoming Someone Students Can Trust in a World That Often Shifts

"They're watching to see if you'll stay. If you'll listen. If you're safe."
— *TCK mentor*

In a world shaped by constant movement, change, and goodbyes, many Third Culture Kids (TCKs) have learned to protect themselves. Before they open up, they're quietly asking:
 "Can I trust you?"
 "Will you still be around?"
 "Do you care enough to stay?"

As a teacher, you hold a sacred opportunity to offer consistency, safety, and genuine connection.

This section helps you cultivate relationships that affirm dignity, build belonging, and honour the unique stories your students carry.

🌍 Why This Matters

In transient communities, trust is the rarest and most healing gift you can offer.

For globally mobile students, relationships often begin with a question mark, not a welcome. They may need to watch you stay before they can believe you care.

The goal isn't to be their best friend — it's to be a safe, steady presence in a world that feels temporary.

Start Small, Go Deep Over Time

TCKs and internationally mobile students often arrive with:
- Guarded hearts shaped by loss
- Hesitancy to form new attachments
- Awareness that adults often move on

Connection doesn't begin with deep talks. It begins with noticing remembering names, showing up consistently, offering gentle space to draw near at their own pace.

Trust grows quietly in the soil of everyday presence.

> **💬 Teacher Insight**
>
> Your consistency teaches more than your charisma.
>
> Every time you keep a promise, show up, or listen without rushing to fix — you're rewriting what trust can feel like.

Trust Builders vs. Trust Blockers

Trust Builders	Trust Blockers
Following through on what you say	Over-promising or forgetting
Listening without fixing or preaching	Giving quick spiritual answers
Remembering small things (like names or stories)	Ignoring their background or minimising identity
Admitting when you're wrong	Acting like you always know best
Protecting their privacy	Sharing personal details or gossip
Noticing when they're "off"	Dismissing or joking away emotions
Including them in small decisions	Talking about them rather than to them

Trust is built drop by drop — but it can be lost in a single moment of carelessness.

Ways to Connect Without Forcing It

- Greet students by name — daily.
- Ask low-pressure questions like, "What's been the best part of your week so far?"
- Use gentle invitations to share — music, art, journaling, photos.
- Participate in their world — join activities instead of standing apart.
- Learn how they express care: through humour, help, or quiet loyalty.
- Respect silence; for many, it's sacred space.

"Connection is built in the quiet moments between tasks, not just the big teaching moments."

📕 Be Aware of Cultural and Emotional Boundaries

In cross-cultural environments, warmth must be paired with wisdom.

What feels friendly to you may feel intrusive, inappropriate, or confusing to your students.

Ask yourself:
- What does respect look like in this culture?
- How do students express comfort, gratitude, or distress?
- What nonverbal cues am I missing?
- How can I adapt my communication without losing authenticity?

Compassion without cultural awareness can cause harm, even when your intentions are good.

In-the-Moment Reflections

Use these prompts when you're unsure how to respond to a student:
- "Is this student pulling away, or just processing?"
- "What might this behaviour be trying to say?"
- "Do I need to fix this, or simply sit with them in it?"
- "How can I build trust without needing a deep talk?"
- "What does safety look like for this student right now?"

Sometimes presence matters more than progress.

✏️ Reflection While You're Overseas

Now that you're living and teaching in a new culture, connection looks different every day. Some moments feel rich and relational; others feel distant or uncertain.

Use these prompts to pause and stay grounded in why you're here — to see, listen, and stay present with the students entrusted to you.

- Where have I seen small signs of trust beginning to grow?

- Who is harder for me to connect with, and why might that be?

- How do I respond when students pull away or test my consistency?

- What assumptions about "connection" am I learning to release?

- How do I care for my own emotional energy while staying available to others?

- Who helps me process relationships in healthy, honest ways?

Connection overseas is rarely instant. It's built in a thousand small, faithful moments — one day, one conversation, one act of noticing at a time.

> 🌱 **Final Thought:**
> Presence Builds Trust — Not Performance
>
> For globally mobile students, safety doesn't come from calm words or grand gestures.
>
> It comes from consistency — from adults who listen, notice, and stay.
>
> You don't need to "connect" in a big, emotional moment.
> You only need to show up every day, see them, and stay.
>
> *"The most powerful teachers are not the loudest — they're the ones who keep showing up."*

Section 8: Creating Space for Belonging

Creating Space for Belonging
Helping Students Feel Seen, Safe, and Significant

"Home isn't always a place. Sometimes it's where someone says, 'I'm glad you're here.'"
— Adult TCK

For Third Culture Kids (TCKs) and globally mobile students, belonging is not a given — it's something they're always trying to piece together.

Their accent might not match their passport. Their stories might stretch across continents.
And inside your classroom, they may quietly wonder:
"Is there space for someone like me here?"

As a teacher overseas, you can't erase what makes students feel different or disconnected but you can create a community where every child is seen, heard, and valued just as they are.

Your classroom can become a place of belonging — even for those who feel they belong nowhere else.

🌍 Why This Matters

Belonging is a core human need. For many globally mobile students, it's also a deep ache. When everything familiar changes friends, routines, languages, and homes they long for connection that feels safe and unconditional.

When you make room for difference, you make room for healing.

Belonging isn't created by programs or policies. It's nurtured through daily acts of presence, respect, and care.

What Belonging Looks Like

Belonging isn't about sameness.
It's about being accepted without having to shrink.

It sounds like:
- "You remembered my name."
- "You asked about my country."
- "You didn't make fun of my accent."
- "You let me say 'I don't know' without shame."
- "You saw me when I was quiet—and didn't push me away."

Belonging happens when students don't have to perform to be accepted.

> 💬 **Teacher Insight**
>
> When students feel safe to be fully themselves, learning becomes freedom not performance.
>
> You don't have to fix their displacement or define their identity.
> Your role is to build a classroom culture that communicates:
> "You belong here — before you achieve, before you adapt."
>
> Every time you slow down to listen, pronounce their name correctly, or protect their dignity in a misunderstanding, you are building a small bridge of belonging.

Honouring Identity in the Multicultural Classroom

TCKs often hold fluid, layered identities. They may:
- Feel connected to multiple cultures — and yet to none fully.
- Struggle to answer, "Where are you from?"
- Adapt behaviour to fit different groups.
- Downplay their background to blend in.
- Feel pressure to align with the dominant culture.

In your classroom, cultural expression can be a strength not something to smooth out.

Ideas to Foster Identity Exploration

- Create a "Where We're From" wall using maps, strings, or photos.
- Invite students to share traditions, foods, or songs — only with consent.
- Encourage storytelling through art, poetry, or music playlists.
- Avoid assuming all students share the same childhood experiences.
- Use open-ended prompts like:
  "Share a place that holds meaning for you."

You don't need to understand every part of their identity you just need to make space for it.

What to Say to Build Belonging

Instead of	Try Saying
"You came from Australia, right?"	"Tell me about the places that feel like home for you."
"Can you explain this holiday to the class?"	"Would you like to share anything about your traditions?"
"Teach us a word from your language!"	"Only if you're comfortable—no pressure."
"You're so different from other students."	"You bring such a unique perspective to our class."

Belonging grows when curiosity replaces assumption.

Belonging Without Pressure

Be careful not to turn a student's cultural background into a class exhibit.
For some, being asked to represent "where they're from" can feel like exposure, not honour.

Instead of spotlighting, offer invitation and choice.
Belonging comes from freedom, not forced inclusion.

✏️ Reflection While You're Overseas

Now that you're living and teaching cross-culturally, belonging looks different for you, too.

Use these reflections to notice where belonging is being built around you:

- Where have I seen students start to relax or laugh freely this week?

- Who still seems to stay on the edges of the classroom community?

- How can I affirm identity without singling someone out?

- What am I learning about how I find belonging in this culture?

- Who helps me see my classroom blind spots about inclusion?

- How might I model belonging for students who are still learning what it feels like?

When you create belonging for others, you often find your own in the process.

> 🌱 **Final Thought:**
> **A Place to Be Fully Themselves**
>
> You may not be able to offer your students a permanent home — but you can give them something just as powerful: a safe space where they feel seen, valued, and at peace being who they are.
>
> *"In a world where they often feel in between, your classroom can be the one place where they finally feel whole."*

Section 9: Navigating Transitions & Goodbyes

Navigating Transitions & Goodbyes
Supporting Students Through Constant Change

"Just when I start to feel safe, someone leaves."
— 13-year-old TCK

In international and mission school settings, change is woven into daily life. Students arrive and leave mid-year. Teachers come and go. Families move countries, sometimes with only a few weeks' notice.

For globally mobile students, this rhythm of arrivals and departures is normal but it's not easy. Each transition carries a subtle cost: another friend gone, another place left behind, another goodbye that's expected to be quick and painless

.As a teacher, you have a powerful opportunity to model a different way one that slows down, honours connection, and helps students process loss instead of burying it.

You can't stop the leaving — but you can help make it matter.

🌍 Why This Matters

Goodbyes are one of the most consistent and least acknowledged parts of a TCK's story. Each move or transition reshapes their sense of identity, belonging, and trust.

Without space to process these moments, many students learn to protect themselves by feeling less—detaching instead of grieving.

As a teacher, you hold the power to help them rewrite that pattern. When you slow down to acknowledge endings and beginnings, you communicate something profound:
- Your story matters. Your feelings are safe here. You don't have to pretend you're fine to be loved.
- Creating space for healthy goodbyes isn't sentimental—it's essential.

It teaches students that relationships can end with care, not avoidance, and that loss can coexist with hope.

The Reality of Transition for TCKs

For most TCKs, transition isn't a one-time event—it's a lifestyle.
They may experience:
- Frequent school changes across continents
- Sudden departures due to visas, instability, or family shifts
- A revolving door of friendships and teachers
- The need to constantly "start over"
- Quiet grief hidden beneath high performance

"Most people assume we're good at goodbyes. We're not—we're just used to them."

This repeated cycle can blur the line between adaptability and exhaustion.
Even those who appear confident may be quietly managing loss, fear, and fatigue.

The Cost of Constant Goodbyes

When transitions go unacknowledged, loss doesn't disappear — it just goes underground.

Common outcomes include:
- Emotional withdrawal or numbness
- Reluctance to form close attachments
- Anxiety or irritability in class
- Difficulty concentrating or completing work

Distrust of adults who "might not stay"

Even students who remain year after year can experience "stayer's grief" — the loneliness of watching others leave while they remain behind.

Grief doesn't only belong to the ones leaving; it also lives in those left behind.

> **Teacher Insight**
>
> Transitions are spiritual as much as emotional. They ask us to let go of what's familiar and to trust that something good can still grow in the in-between.
>
> Your role isn't to fix grief — it's to recognize and dignify it.
>
> When you create small rituals of farewell or acknowledgment, you communicate that connection mattered.
>
> Students learn that endings can be meaningful, not just painful.

How You Can Help

Acknowledge Every Transition
- Don't minimize or rush through goodbyes.
- Make time for closure — even if it's simple.
- Remember: every arrival is also a goodbye to somewhere else.
- Name both beginnings and endings in your class rhythm.

"Welcome weeks" are just as sacred as "farewell weeks."

Use the RAFT Model
(Developed by David C. Pollock & Ruth Van Reken, authors of Third Culture Kids: Growing Up Among Worlds)

Step	Meaning	Application in the Classroom
R – Reconciliation	Resolve conflicts before departure.	Encourage students to write a note or have a calm conversation if something feels unresolved.
A – Affirmation	Say the good out loud.	Create gratitude circles or peer notes. "One thing I'll miss about you is…"
F – Farewells	Say goodbye to people, places, pets, and routines.	Invite students to name what they'll miss — not just who.
T – Think Destination	Talk about what's next, without pressure.	Help students visualize and pray for what's ahead, holding space for hope and fear together.

Normalise the Grief of Change

- Grief looks different for every student. Some cry, some act out, some go silent.
- Help them understand that sadness is not weakness — it's a sign of connection.
- Say things like:
  "Missing people means you loved them well."
  "You can feel sad and still have a good day."
  "Grief doesn't always look like tears; sometimes it's quiet."
  "It's okay if you're not ready to say goodbye yet."

Your empathy gives permission for students to feel what they've been taught to suppress.

Practical Ideas for the Classroom

- Transition Wall or Tree – Create a space for names/photos of those arriving or leaving.
- Memory Books – Encourage notes, drawings, or affirmations for departing classmates.
- Goodbye Circles – Simple, intentional time to speak gratitude and blessing.
- Hello & Goodbye Board – A visible reminder that change is part of the community's story.
- "I Remember…" Letters – Invite students to capture memories or lessons they'll carry forward.
- Continuity Rituals – Light a candle, plant a tree, or share a song to mark endings and beginnings.

These rituals remind students that relationships matter, even when they change form.

Cultural Sensitivity in Transitions

In some cultures, direct emotional expression like crying or hugging goodbye may feel uncomfortable or inappropriate. Instead of assuming what closure should look like, offer options: writing, art, or silent reflection.

Ask yourself:
- What does "goodbye" look like in this culture?
- How do people here express gratitude or grief?
- What tone feels respectful for farewells — public celebration or quiet acknowledgment?
- Adapt your approach so it honours both the student's needs and the host culture's rhythm.

✏️ Reflection While You're Overseas

Transitions don't just affect your students — they shape you too.
Living overseas means continually saying goodbye, even as you help others do the same.

Use these prompts to reflect honestly and stay emotionally grounded:

- How do I personally respond to endings — do I rush them, avoid them, or linger too long?

- What rituals help me process my own goodbyes well?

- Have I made space for both leaving and staying students to express their emotions?

- Who helps me process the emotional weight of turnover and loss?

- How do I keep showing up with hope in a place of constant change?

When you learn to say goodbye well, you teach your students that endings can be sacred, not just sad.

> 🌱 **Final Thought:**
> **Saying Goodbye Is Part of Loving Well**
>
> For globally mobile students, goodbyes are inevitable but they don't have to be empty.
>
> With empathy, structure, and intentionality, each farewell can become a reminder that connection was real and love was worth it.
>
> *"You can't stop the leaving—but you can help make it matter."*

Section 10: Caring for Yourself

Caring for Yourself
Sustainability for the Long Haul in Cross-Cultural Teaching

"You can't pour from an empty cup—but in international work, we often try."
— Cross-Cultural Educator

Teaching overseas can be deeply fulfilling but it can also be quietly exhausting. You're balancing lesson planning with culture shock, navigating new norms, and holding emotional space for students who are grieving, adjusting, and watching you to see how stability looks in motion.

It's easy to assume that resilience means endurance but resilience is sustained by rest, support, and rhythm.

To care well for others, you need to care well for yourself.

You can't be a steady presence for others if you never let yourself stop moving.

This section offers practical insight for staying grounded, emotionally healthy, and spiritually alive while serving in complex cross-cultural contexts.

🌍 Why This Matters

When teachers burn out, the loss goes beyond the classroom it ripples through relationships, mentorships, and community life.

In international and mission contexts, where home and work often blur, many educators quietly carry heavy emotional loads while believing that self-care is selfish.

But sustainability is not self-indulgence; it's stewardship. Your wellbeing directly shapes the atmosphere your students live and learn in.

Healthy teachers model what it means to be whole showing students that strength and rest can coexist, and that even the most devoted servant still needs space to breathe.

"The most powerful lesson you teach may not come from your curriculum, but from how you live your limits with grace."

Why It's Easy to Burn Out Overseas

Cross-cultural educators and missionaries often live within overlapping worlds work, community, and ministry all intertwined. The result? No clear off switch.

You may be:
- Working and living in the same space blurring professional and personal boundaries
- Separated from close friends, mentors, or your home church
- In environments where rest isn't seen as essential or "spiritual"
- Carrying students' emotional or faith burdens as your own
- Feeling guilty for needing support when others seem to have it tougher

"Just because you're capable doesn't mean you're coping well."

Teacher Insight:

The greatest threat to longevity overseas isn't cultural confusion it's compassion fatigue.

You were called to give, not to disappear. Healthy teachers model sustainability, not self-sacrifice.

The Core Needs to Monitor
(Adapted from cross-cultural resilience research and Pollock & Van Reken's TCK wellbeing framework)

Need	Neglected Signs	Healthy Responses
Rest	Fatigue, irritability, emotional flatness	Schedule non-negotiable downtime; include digital rest.
Connection	Loneliness, numbness, isolation	Prioritise regular calls, mentorship, or small community.
Purpose	Cynicism, overworking, burnout	Reconnect with your "why"; revisit your original sense of call.
Joy	Loss of laughter or curiosity	Re-engage creativity music, reading, art, play.
Spiritual Rhythm	Dryness, guilt, disengagement	Explore faith practices that meet you where you are, not where you "should be."

Resilience grows when needs are noticed before they become crises

Healthy Rhythms to Anchor You

Weekly Rest / Sabbath: Even if your host culture doesn't model it, keep it sacred.

Journaling or Creative Expression: Capture what you're learning and feeling.

Nature & Movement: Take walks, stretch, breathe deeply — reconnect with creation.

Safe People: Find one or two trusted friends you can speak openly with.

Professional Debriefing: Mission or school counsellors can help carry the load.

Spiritual Care: Anchor in Scripture, silence, prayer, or familiar worship rhythms.

Gratitude Practice: End each week noting what sustained you, not just what drained you.

Rest is not reward for finishing the work — it's what makes the work possible.

Warning Signs You Shouldn't Ignore

- Persistent exhaustion, dread, or disrupted sleep
- Emotional detachment or irritability toward students
- Losing joy in teaching or connection
- Feeling hopeless, numb, or alone
- Increasing escapism, cynicism, or "auto-pilot" living

If these signs persist, reach out for help — whether to a counsellor, supervisor, or trusted peer.

You're not weak for needing support. You're human — and healing often begins with honesty.

Stewardship, Not Selfishness

"Self-care is not indulgence — it's stewardship."

In faith-based settings, self-care can feel self-centered. But burnout doesn't make you more spiritual — it just makes you unavailable.

When you care for yourself, you're honouring God's creation in you, and ensuring you can continue to serve with integrity and joy.

The care you extend to others should begin with how you treat yourself.

 Reflection While You're Overseas

You're in the middle of the work — tired, hopeful, still learning.
Take a moment to pause and listen inwardly.

- What fills my cup — emotionally, physically, and spiritually?

- Where am I feeling most drained right now?

- Who checks in on me regularly, and how do I respond?

- Do I create the same care for myself that I offer my students?

- What might rest look like in this season — and what keeps me from embracing it?

- How might I trust God's pace, not my performance?

The healthiest teachers are those who learn to receive as deeply as they give.

> 🌱 **Final Thought**
> **Self-Care Is Not Selfish — It's Stewardship**
>
> Your wellbeing matters — not because you're indispensable, but because you're human.
>
> You don't serve best when you're perfect; you serve best when you're present, rested, and real.
>
> *"Let the care you give others start with you."*
>
> In the long arc of teaching and mission, sustainability isn't found in strength it's found in rhythm.

Conclusion: Teaching Beyond Borders

Conclusion: Teaching Beyond Borders
The Journey Doesn't End When the Term Does

"To teach cross-culturally is to live in the tension between what you know and what you're still learning."

Teaching overseas is not simply about geography it's about growth.

You began this journey with a suitcase and a calling, perhaps unsure of what awaited you. Along the way, you've encountered classrooms full of accents, laughter, grief, and grace. You've been stretched, humbled, inspired, and sometimes undone.

The borders you crossed are more than lines on a map — they are thresholds of the heart.

What You've Carried, What You've Given

In this journey, you've discovered that teaching is not only about information, but formation.

You've learned that faith can take new forms in unfamiliar soil, that love translates even when language doesn't, and that humility often teaches the deepest lessons of all.

You have:
- Listened to stories that changed how you see the world
- Helped students discover their identity between cultures
- Made space for grief, laughter, and healing
- Learned to stay steady when everything shifts

You've modeled not perfection, but presence — the steady, quiet kind that tells students: you are seen, you are known, you matter.

Teaching as a Global Calling

Whether you return home or continue across borders, your work carries ripples far beyond the classroom walls.

Every act of patience, every moment of kindness, every story you've honored has contributed to a larger story — one of reconciliation, courage, and hope.

Teaching beyond borders is not about going everywhere.
It's about living with open hands wherever you are.

As global educators, we are called to embody both truth and tenderness, learning to see God's image reflected in every culture, every student, and every story.

✏️ Reflection: A Final Pause

- What have you learned about yourself that surprised you?

- What have your students taught you about grace and resilience?

- How has this experience expanded your view of God, of home, of belonging?

- What rhythms or relationships will sustain you in the next season?

- How will you continue to live "in the in-between" with faith and courage?

Every ending in this life of movement is also a new beginning.

> 🌱 **Final Thought**
>
> May you continue to teach with curiosity,
> to listen before speaking,
> to rest before breaking,
> and to see every student — every story — as sacred ground.
>
> Wherever you go next, may you carry the lessons of the in-between:
> humility, compassion, resilience, and love.
>
> Teaching beyond borders begins inside the heart —
> and it never truly ends.

Resources & Recommended Reading

Understanding TCKs & Global Mobility

- Third Culture Kids: Growing Up Among Worlds — David C. Pollock, Ruth E. Van Reken & Michael Pollock (Nicholas Brealey, 2017)
- Misunderstood: The Impact of Growing Up Overseas in the 21st Century — Tanya Crossman (Summertime Publishing, 2016)
- Belonging Everywhere & Nowhere — Lois Bushong (Mango Tree Intercultural Services, 2013)
- Raising Up a Generation of Healthy Third Culture Kids — Lauren Wells (Summertime Publishing, 2020)
- Unstacking Your Grief Tower — Lauren Wells (TCK Training Press, 2022)
- The Grief Tower: A Practical Guide to Supporting TCKs Through Grief and Loss — Lauren Wells (TCK Training Press, 2020)

Education & Emotional Wellbeing

- Helping Children Succeed — Paul Tough (Mariner Books, 2016)
- The Whole-Brain Child — Daniel J. Siegel & Tina Payne Bryson (Delacorte Press, 2011)
- Atlas of the Heart — Brené Brown (Random House, 2021)
- The Invisible String — Patrice Karst (DeVorss & Company, 2000)

Faith & Cross-Cultural Service

- Cross-Cultural Servanthood: Serving the World in Christlike Humility — Duane Elmer (IVP Books, 2006)
- Strengthening the Soul of Your Leadership — Ruth Haley Barton (IVP Books, 2008)
- Liturgy of the Ordinary — Tish Harrison Warren (IVP Books, 2016)
- Serving Well: Help for the Wannabe, Newbie, or Weary Cross-Cultural Worker — Elizabeth & Jonathan Trotter (Self-published, 2019)

Practical Tools for Teachers Overseas

- The Culture Map — Erin Meyer (PublicAffairs, 2014)
- Foreign to Familiar — Sarah A. Lanier (McDougal Publishing, 2000)

8 In the In-Between

www.ingramcontent.com/pod-product-compliance
Lightning Source LLC
Chambersburg PA
CBHW081417300426
44109CB00020BA/2359